Books by Tim Barker

Anticipating the Return of Christ

At Your Feet

Called Camp 2025

End Times

God's Revelation and Your Future

It's Not All About Sitting at the Head Table

Mighty Men of Courage from the Bible

My Jesus Journey

My Jesus Journey: Crescendo

My Jesus Journey: Glissando

My Jesus Journey: Rhapsody

Names of God

Open Doors

Our Privilege of Joy

Reflecting Christ Through the Fruit of the Spirit

The Authentic Christian: Revealing Christ through the Fruit of the Spirit

The Call of Ephesians

The Lord with Us

The Twelve: Taking Up the Mantle of Christ

The Vision of Nehemiah: God's Plan for Righteous Living

Truth, Love & Redemption: The Holy Spirit for Today

Unified Church

Your Invitation to Christ

Discovering
GOD
in the
Secret
Places

Discovering GOD in the Secret Places

Tim R. Barker, D. Min.

Network Pastor/Superintendent
South Texas Ministry Network

DISCOVERING GOD IN THE SECRET PLACES, Barker, Tim.

1st ed.

Unless otherwise noted, Scriptures are taken from the New International Version (NIV): Scripture taken from The Holy Bible, New International Version ®. Copyright© 1973, 1978, 1984, 2011 by Biblica, Inc.™. Used by permission of Zondervan.

ISBN: 979-8-9924875-3-4

Dedication

In the early days of my youth ministry, I had a heartfelt conversation with Michelle, a young girl in our church who had already endured significant loss in her short life. She was wrestling with deep questions about God's existence and why He allowed such painful tragedies to touch her world. I didn't have all the answers. All I could do was gently point her to Deuteronomy 29:29 and pray she would find peace in accepting some things as part of God's hidden wisdom—and choose to trust what He has revealed in His Word.

Her response caught me off guard. With sincere resolve, she said, "Pastor Tim, when I get to heaven, I'm going to ask!" I thought that was a completely honest—and valid—response from a young teenager trying to make sense of her pain. But then came a sacred moment. With tears rolling down her cheeks, Michelle softly added, "I suppose … when I get to Heaven, it really won't matter."

That moment marked me. So, I dedicate this book to Michelle—for teaching me a profound truth early in my ministry journey:

I don't always need to have all the answers. Deuteronomy 29:29 gives us that grace.

Tim R. Barker

Contents

Introduction

Unanswered prayer.

The job loss. Fractured relationships. The times we pray and feel like Heaven is closed.

The Word reveals to us that we will never have all the answers. God has set boundaries on our knowledge. We don't (and shouldn't be able to) control the timing of what happens to us as we live out each day.

We don't have the wisdom to make the choices that are good for us. What seems right and appropriate for us, our families, and those we affect is based on feelings, circumstances, and the emotions that drive us to react rather than to reason.

Yet, God is working around us all the time. We cry, "Where are you, God?" He whispers to us, "Slow down, and you will find me."

Some answers will never be ours. That's when we must release "control" and base our faith in "trust." That's when we allow our divine Father to work in our lives according to His wisdom and not our sense of urgency.

And that's the Mystery ... of being a Christian, of living a life based on the Word of God, of choosing Christ instead of the world.

As you read this book, challenge yourself. Choose Wonder over Worry, bask in God's Season, and let the calendar of your life be written by the One who delivers us from a life of sin and shame.

Choose to trust in God, for He is the only one deserving of our eternal adoration.

— I —

The Mystery Begins

_____

The Pull of the Unknown

The secret things belong to the Lord our God, but the things revealed belong to us and to our children forever ...

— Deuteronomy 29:29 —

HAVE YOU ever found yourself staring up at the night sky, letting your mind drift past the stars? No matter how advanced our telescopes are, there are still corners of the universe we'll never see.

One summer evening, I walked on the beach with my daughters trying to count the stars. My oldest asked me a question that stopped me cold:

"Dad, does God live behind the stars?"

I opened my mouth, ready to answer. But I closed it just as quickly, because sometimes the best thing we can say is:

"I don't know. But I trust the One who does."

We crave answers. But life, faith, and God, Himself, often meet us with mystery.

The Boundaries of Knowing

When Moses spoke to the Israelites on the plains of Moab, they stood on the threshold of the Promised Land. An entire generation had been raised in the wilderness and were now called to trust God for the next unknown.

Moses reminded them that not everything was theirs to know.

It was a line in the sand. Some things God had revealed: His laws, His instructions, His covenant promises. And some things He had kept hidden.

The same line runs through our lives. We have a thousand questions:

- Why did this happen?

- When will this change?

- How will this work out?

- Why me?

Deuteronomy 29:29 teaches us that God holds secrets — not to tease us, but to protect us. Some things are simply too big for us to carry. He holds the unseen so that we can walk in trust.

A Hidden Thread

Consider Joseph, the dreamer who was sold by his brothers, wrongly imprisoned, and forgotten by those he helped. For years, his life must have felt like a cruel joke. What did the dreams mean now? Where was God?

Only later, looking back from the palace, did Joseph understand the hidden thread:

> *You meant evil against me, but God meant it for good ...*
>
> — Genesis 50:20 —

The secret things often make sense only in hindsight. And sometimes not even then ... but always in eternity.

The Garden Temptation

In the garden, the serpent offered Eve something God never did:

You will be like God, knowing good and evil.

— Genesis 3:5 —

The original temptation was not the fruit. It was the hunger to know what was forbidden.

We are not that different today. We surf the internet for answers to questions the soul can't uncover. We push for information to make us feel in control. But the ache to know everything can drag us away from the peace of trusting the One who knows it all.

Modern Restlessness

I once spoke with a young man who was unraveling under the weight of his unanswered prayers. He said:

"If I just knew why God let this happen, I'd be okay."

But that wasn't true. Knowing why rarely brings peace. Only knowing Who does.

Mystery isn't God's punishment. It's His protection. He invites us to trade our obsession with answers for the peace of His presence.

Faith in the Dark

Faith does not require full sight. It thrives in the dark. It grows in mystery. It deepens when we realize God's secrets are not hidden *from* us but *for* us. They are treasures tucked away until the time is right.

Like seeds buried underground, some truths sprout only when our hearts are ready to handle them.

Walking the Edge

I think of Abraham, told to leave everything familiar for a land he couldn't see. Or Mary, visited by an angel, overshadowed by mystery, and carrying a promise that made no sense in human logic.

These stories echo the same theme: God does not lay it all out in advance. He invites us to step into what we know and trust Him with what we don't.

Practical Trust: How to Live with Secret Things

Acknowledge the Boundary

Pray honestly: "Lord, I release what belongs to You alone. Help me focus on what You have revealed."

Hold the Mystery Open-Handed

Instead of demanding clarity, ask for deeper faith. Say: "I trust You in the dark."

Keep Walking in What You Do Know

Obey the simple things: love God, love people, do justice, love mercy, and walk humbly.

Speak Peace Over Your Mind

When questions torment you, anchor yourself in Scripture:

You will keep in perfect peace those whose minds are steadfast, because they trust in You.

— Isaiah 26:3 —

A Hidden Jewel

I once heard an old pastor say:

"God tells us enough to trust Him and withholds enough to keep us close."

That's the hidden jewel of mystery. It pulls us deeper into relationship. It keeps us searching, listening, and leaning in.

Chapter I

The Mystery Begins

Reflection Questions

What secret thing have you been demanding an answer for?

How would your heart change if you trusted that some answers are safe in His hands?

What part of your life needs the peace that comes from letting go?

A Closing Prayer

Father, I surrender my need to know.

I trust that the secret things belong to You and that the things You reveal are enough for today.

Strengthen my faith where I can't see.

Keep my eyes fixed on Your goodness when my mind craves answers.

I trust You with the mystery. Amen.

Challenge Yourself

Write down one question that has haunted you and place it in your Bible at Deuteronomy 29:29.

Every time you see it, whisper:

"This belongs to the Lord."

Write down what the Lord reveals to you and share it with like-minded Christians.

— 2 —

Hidden in Plain Sight

The Everyday Secret

Call to me and I will answer you and tell you great and unsearchable things you do not know.

— Jeremiah 33:3 —

Hidden in Plain Sight

ONE AFTERNOON, I sat across from an elderly woman at a church potluck. Between bites of her famous potato salad, she said something that stuck with me:

"Sometimes the greatest miracles are the ones we don't notice until much later."

I didn't grasp it then, but now I see how true it is. God often hides treasures in the open, scattered among the moments we think are ordinary.

The Kingdom Is Like ...

When Jesus wanted to describe the Kingdom of God, He didn't reach for a complicated theological scroll. He reached for everyday things: seeds, yeast, pearls, and fields.

"The Kingdom of heaven is like a mustard seed ... a hidden treasure ... a merchant looking for fine pearls." (Matt. 13:31-32)

These images invite us to look closer. They whisper that the sacred often wears ordinary clothes.

A Story in the Checkout Line

I once stood in line at the grocery store, annoyed at the person in front of me for paying with loose change. I muttered under my breath, shifting impatiently, until I caught her eyes — tired, apologetic, and embarrassed.

In that moment, God's Spirit nudged me: "Slow down. See her."

I paid the remaining few dollars and walked her to her car. She told me about her sick husband at home. We prayed right there in the parking lot.

It was an ordinary Tuesday, but Heaven had been hidden right in front of me.

Missing the Obvious

We pray for signs and wonders. We ask for confirmation. But sometimes we miss the answers because we expect them to arrive wrapped in the spectacular.

Meanwhile, God slips them into conversations, interruptions, delays, and the smallest kindnesses.

He hides things in plain sight so only those who look with open eyes will find them.

Jesus at the Table

Think of the road to Emmaus. The resurrected Jesus walked beside two disciples for miles. They didn't recognize Him until He broke bread at the table.

He was right there the whole time.

How many times has God walked with us — hidden in plain sight — while we were too distracted to notice?

The Call to Pay Attention

Brother Lawrence, the humble monk, called it practicing the presence of God. For him, washing dishes was holy. Peeling potatoes became prayer.

Nothing was beneath God's presence. Nothing was too small to carry a secret.

What if you looked at your daily routine — emails, dishes, traffic lights — as places where God might be whispering?

Your Life as a Parable

The Bible is full of hidden stories:

- Ruth gleaning in a field

- David in a pasture

- Mary at a well

- Peter mending nets

God met them where they least expected Him — in fields, kitchens, workplaces, and on shorelines.

Your life is no different. Heaven's secrets are scattered through your daily life — hidden in plain sight.

How to Find Them

Slow Down

Pause in your routine. Watch for the sacred in the small events that take place all around you. Be perceptive.

Listen for the Nudge

When you feel that holy pull to speak, help, or pray, then do it. That's how hidden things come into view.

Stay Present

Put down the phone. Look someone in the eye. Ask the second question, the one that opens the door to the real story.

One Hidden Moment

I think about the man in Acts 3, the beggar at the temple gate called Beautiful. How many people stepped over him every day? Peter and John did not just see a lame man. They saw a moment Heaven had hidden in plain sight.

One moment of attention turned into a miracle that rippled through Jerusalem.

Chapter 2

Hidden in Plain Sight

Reflection Questions

Where in your daily routine might God be waiting for you to notice Him?

Who have you overlooked that might be carrying a hidden story?

What ordinary thing can you see differently this week?

Hidden in Plain Sight

Reflection Questions

A Closing Prayer

Lord, open my eyes to see the treasure hidden in my everyday life.

Slow me down when I rush past the sacred.

Give me courage to pause, to notice, to act when You whisper.

May I never miss the miracles hidden in plain sight. Amen.

Challenge Yourself

Pick one ordinary task, like your commute or washing dishes, and pray:

"Lord, show me something hidden here."

Write down what you see or sense that the Lord has shown you. Share it with someone to encourage them to also look for God in the small, everyday parts of life.

— 3 —

The Limits of Knowing

When Answers Don't Answer

For now we see only a reflection as in a mirror; then we shall see face to face. Now I know in part; then I shall know fully, even as I am fully known.

— I Corinthians 13:12 —

A FEW YEARS AGO, I sat in a hospital waiting room with a family who had just lost their father. The room was thick with quiet sobs and unspoken questions.

Finally, one of the sons looked at me and said:

"Pastor, why did God let this happen? We prayed. We believed."

In that moment, I wished I had a clear, neat answer, a theology that could stitch their grief back together.

But all I could do was sit beside them in the ache of not knowing.

Some things, I've learned, will never be solved on this side of Heaven.

What We Can't Google

We live in an age where ignorance is seen as failure. Type your question into a search bar, and thousands of answers appear. We crave information because it makes us feel in control.

Yet for all our brilliance, there are walls we cannot climb:

The doctor who shrugs, "We don't know why this happened."

The prayers that hang in the air without explanation.

The future that won't reveal itself, no matter how hard we plan.

Knowledge is a gift, but it has limits. It's the mystery of life that reminds us that we are human and that God is not.

Job's Story: Wrestling with Silence

The book of Job is a masterclass in unanswered questions. Job lost everything: his family, wealth, health, and even his reputation. His friends tried to explain it:

"You must have sinned."

"God is punishing you."

But Job knew better. He wanted a face-to-face encounter with the Almighty.

When God finally spoke, He didn't explain why. Instead, He asked Job a question:

"Where were you when I laid the earth's foundation?"

Job's demands for answers dissolved into worship of the great and mighty God of all creation. He saw what I'm trying to show you, that the secret things belong to the Lord, and that is enough.

The Gift in the Gaps

Why does God leave gaps in our understanding?

Because faith lives there.

If you could explain every pain, every mystery, or every closed door, you would have no need to place your trust in the God of the heavens.

Faith is forged in the unknown. Hope grows best when life batters us, and we see only the shadows that try to envelop us. Then, rather than giving in, we choose to hold onto the Light.

Stories in the Dark

Corrie ten Boom survived the horrors of a Nazi concentration camp. She wrote later:

"When a train goes through a tunnel and it gets dark, you don't throw away the ticket and jump off. You sit still and trust the engineer."

So often, we want to bail when mystery comes. God leads us through a dark time in our life, perhaps a health diagnosis or a natural disaster … even a relationship failure, and the reason why is lost to us.

Here's what we must understand: Mystery is not a wall to break through. It's a place to meet the One who holds all things together. It is time to place our trust in Him.

Rather than get trapped in our pain and lack of understanding, it's important to look to the One who leads us out the other side.

When "Why" Becomes "Who"

I remember praying for a young woman with stage four cancer. We begged for healing. When she passed away, I wrestled with my lack of understanding.

Why didn't God heal her?

Her husband told me, "I don't know why she wasn't healed here. But I know Who holds her now. That's enough for me."

Sometimes, our greatest faith is not found in the answers we search for but in finding our resting spot in the God who doesn't owe us anything yet chooses to love us anyway.

Living Humbly

We must take a page from the life of the great prophets of the Old Testament:

Ask the big questions but hold the answers we search for loosely. Dig deep into the important matters of life but bow low to the God of creation when the answers come our way.

Faith isn't about closing the gaps with our own knowledge, decisions, or certainty. Faith isn't about proof, reasoning, or understanding.

It's about trusting the One who promises that one day we'll understand the cause, have our answers, and discover the "why" when we see Him face to face.

Practical Ways to Rest in the Unknown

Name Your Questions

Write them down. Talk to God about them honestly. He's not threatened by your doubts.

Trust His Character

What you don't know must bow to what you do know: He is good. He is near. He is love.

Live the Revealed Things

Focus on what He has made clear: Love well. Forgive. Pray. Serve. Be faithful today.

Chapter 3

The Limits of Knowing

Reflection Questions

What is one mystery you've demanded an answer for that you may never have in this life?

How does it feel to admit you don't know?

What part of God's character can anchor you when answers won't come?

A Closing Prayer

Lord, I confess that sometimes I want answers more than I want trust.

Teach me to rest in Your wisdom when mine runs out.

Help me worship in the gaps, believe when I can't see, and hold tightly to Your goodness when the secret things stay secret. Amen.

Challenge Yourself

Write down a "Why?" question you can't answer.

Underneath it, write:

"The secret things belong to the Lord."

Every time this question returns to your thoughts, and you find yourself in a time of confusion, repeat this sentence quietly to yourself:

"I choose to trust in You, anyway."

— 4 —

When God Whispers

The Volume of God

After the earthquake came a fire, but the Lord was not in the fire. And after the fire came a gentle whisper.

— I Kings 19:12 —

WHEN WE think of the voice of God, we often imagine thunder, lightning, and booming declarations ringing out across the skies.

We picture burning bushes and parting seas, with the storm-crossed heavens painting God's presence above us.

But what if the clearest things God wants to say to us are spoken softly ... so softly they can only be heard by a heart tuned to the whispered voice of the Mighty One?

The Story of Elijah

Elijah knew what it was to stand in the thunder. He called fire down from Heaven, defeated false prophets, and outran a king's chariot. Yet, soon after, he found himself alone and afraid, hiding in a cave.

He longed for a dramatic word from God. He waited for God's shout to override and silence his fear.

Instead, the Bible says:

The wind tore the mountains apart, but the Lord was not in the wind.

An earthquake shook the ground, but the Lord was not in the quake.

A fire burned fiercely, but the Lord was not in the fire.

And then came the gentle whisper.

The Power of a Whisper

A whisper means you must come close to hear it.

It requires stillness, quiet, and attentiveness. A whisper is personal, a message meant for the one willing to lean in.

God still whispers today, but the noise of our world drowns Him out. The cacophony of modern living silences the whispers we can no longer discern.

The Loud World vs. the Quiet God

We live in an age of notifications, constant music, endless conversation, and screens screaming for our attention. Silence often feels uncomfortable, even threatening.

A new trend for airplane flight is "rawdogging," when a passenger intentionally does nothing and, instead, embraces a lack of distraction. Essentially, they listen to the whispers of life, the quietness around them, and soak it all in.

Yet, in our busy world of social media and constant information overload, these are the people who seem "odd" or "different."

We need to realize that the secrets of God are often hidden in the hush of the quiet moments, the whispers that can be heard only in life's still moments, and the introspective look into what God desires to say to us.

We can choose a loud world or a quiet God. We cannot embrace both at the same time.

How Jesus Modeled Silence

Jesus, the Son of God, often withdrew to lonely places. In the early morning, before sunrise, He slipped away to pray. In the garden, before His arrest, He prayed alone while His friends slept.

He showed us that sacred secrets are revealed when we get quiet enough to listen.

Learning to Hear the Whisper

When was the last time you sat in quiet stillness, without music, without a screen, and without an agenda?

Just listening?

For many, silence is unfamiliar ground. But it's in the quiet times and the stillness that God's whispers echo the loudest.

A Story: The Unexpected Nudge

I once sat in my car after a long day, with the engine off, feeling exhausted. No music poured in over the speakers, and I had my phone turned off. It was just me, the dashboard, and the faint tick of the cooling engine.

In that silence, I felt a simple phrase in my heart:

"Call your brother."

I hadn't spoken to him in weeks. I almost brushed it off, but I made the call.

He was at a breaking point, overwhelmed, and ready to give up on everything. We talked for hours that night. That whisper that *I chose to listen to* saved him from the edge.

Would I have heard it with the radio blaring? No. Would I have listened if my phone had been playing one of my favorite podcasts? Absolutely not.

God still speaks. But He rarely shouts. We must choose to live our lives in a way that allows His whispers to be heard.

Practicing Holy Stillness

Create Space

Find five minutes today to sit in silence. No music. No list. Just be still.

Listen with Expectation

Ask: "Lord, is there something You want to say to me?" Then wait.

Write What You Sense

It may be a word, an image, a verse, or a name. Record it. Test it against His Word.

When Silence Speaks

Sometimes, the whisper is not words but a settled peace, an idea for someone else, or a gentle correction.

The softest words can change the loudest storms inside of you. Let God speak to you, learn to listen and hear His voice, and your life will be changed.

Chapter 4

When God Whispers

Reflection Questions

When was the last time you heard God whisper something to you?

What noise do you need to silence to hear Him more clearly?

Where can you create space this week for holy stillness?

A Closing Prayer

Lord, quiet my heart so I can hear Your whisper.

Teach me to turn down the world's noise and tune my ear to Your Spirit.

May Your gentle voice guide me, correct me, and remind me that You are near. Amen.

Challenge Yourself

Schedule a "whisper walk" with God.

Make it a walk with no music, no podcast ... just you, God, and open ears.

Ask God to speak. When He does, take the time to listen.

Write down what you sense ... whether it comes to you in words or a feeling that sweeps over you. Put in in your Bible and revisit it during your daily devotions.

— 5 —

The Treasure of Trust

The Weight of What We Don't Know

Trust in the Lord with all your heart and lean not on your own understanding; in all your ways submit to him, and he will make your paths straight.

— Proverbs 3:5-6 —

HAVE YOU ever lain awake at night rehearsing every what if? Our minds race through questions:

What if it doesn't work out?

What if I fail?

What if God doesn't come through?

So often, what burdens us most isn't what we know; it's what we don't. In the darkness, trust becomes the treasure we didn't know we needed.

The Picture of a Seed

Jesus compared trust to a seed planted in the soil. It's hidden, unseen, and silent in the dark. From the surface, it looks like nothing is happening.

But beneath, life is unfolding.

When you trust God with the secret things, you bury your fear in His faithfulness. You plant your questions in His goodness.

And you wait, believing that in the dark places, something holy is growing.

A Story from the Waiting Room

I once sat with a young couple in a fertility clinic. Years of unanswered prayers had brought them to that cold hallway with white walls and hushed voices.

They told me:

"Pastor, we don't know if we'll ever have a child. We don't understand the why of our infertility. But we've decided to place our trust in Him and let Him write our story. We've come to understand that it's not whether we get an answer but whether we choose to place our faith in Him."

Years later, they did have a child. But they told me that the real miracle wasn't the baby, it was the trust that bloomed in their lives during the waiting. They learned that even during the hard times, placing their trust in God carried them through.

Control vs. Trust

The greatest rival to trust is control. We micromanage outcomes. We search symptoms online until we're sick with worry. We draft backup plans for our backup plans.

But every time we choose control over trust, we tighten our grip on what only God can hold.

Sometimes, trusting God feels like letting go of the only rope we have, only to find we're resting in the hands that never fail us: God's hands.

When the Secret Stays Secret

What if the answer never comes? What if the door stays shut?

Real trust does not depend on the outcome but on the One who knows the outcome.

Shadrach, Meshach, and Abednego said to the king:

"Our God is able to deliver us. But even if He does not, we will not bow."

Trust says:

"God, I know You can. But even if You don't, I know You are good."

How to Treasure Trust

Choose Daily Release

Pray daily: "Lord, I release what I can't control. I trust You with it today."

Remember Past Faithfulness

Look back. Remember times He came through when you didn't see a way. Let yesterday's faithfulness feed today's trust.

Speak Trust Out Loud

When fear rises, speak trust out loud: "I trust You, God. I trust You with what I don't see."

A Note on Pain

Trust doesn't mean you pretend it doesn't hurt. Trust means you bring the hurt to the One who can hold it. The tears are holy. The waiting is holy. The mystery is holy ... because it's kept by a holy God.

Chapter 5

The Treasure of Trust

Reflection Questions

Where are you tempted to exercise control instead of trust?

What is one buried seed you need to believe is growing in the dark?

What does it look like to say: "Even if He does not answer, still I will trust Him"?

A Closing Prayer

Lord, I confess I cling to control when trust feels too risky.

I loosen my grip today. I bury my questions in Your goodness.

I believe that what I can't see is safe with You.

Grow my trust in the soil of mystery.

Let my life show that You are trustworthy. Amen.

Challenge Yourself

Each morning, pray:

"Lord, I trust You with [name your worry].
I choose surrender over control."

Write down what shifts inside you by the end of the week.

Be prepared to share your "shifts" with a trusted Christian believer.

— 6 —

Revelation in Seasons

The Ache for "When"

There is a time for everything, and a season for every activity under the heavens.

— Ecclesiastes 3:1 —

IF YOU'VE ever planted a seed, you know the test of waiting. The seed disappears under the dirt, unseen and silent. Days of watching for new growth pass without a sign that anything's different.

Nothing breaks through the soil's surface. You water the dry ground. You wait with bated breath. You hope each morning to see a change.

Faith is like that. So are God's secret things. Some revelations do not come on demand.

They arrive in seasons.

God's Calendar vs. Ours

We love instant answers. We microwave meals, scroll for headlines, or tap a screen for next-day delivery.

But Heaven doesn't work that way. God works in seasons, not seconds. There's no "instant" God for us to find, no way to "scroll" to the blessing we want, and we certainly can't "tap" the giant screen in the sky when we feel He isn't coming through fast enough.

His timing frustrates us because it refuses to be manipulated. But if you look back, you'll see that each time you received an answer to prayer, it was right on time.

Habakkuk's Frustration

The prophet Habakkuk cried out: "How long, Lord?" He saw injustice and silence. He wanted immediate action. God answered:

Though it linger, wait for it; it will certainly come and will not delay.

— Habakkuk 2:3 —

To us, the wait feels like a delay. To God, it's preparation.

A Story of Waiting

I once met a man who spent ten years praying for reconciliation with his estranged father. For a decade, there was nothing but silence. Then, out of nowhere, he received a phone call.

When he picked up the phone, he heard a weeping voice speaking to him. His father was on the other end, now an old man who wanted to say:

"I'm sorry."

The wait may have seemed pointless, for during our time of waiting, it's easy to question why God doesn't bring reconciliation.

Perhaps the years even felt wasted. The young man didn't share that with me.

What he did share was this:

When the door opened, it was clear that God had been working, even though the young man's eyes couldn't see the hand of God in his father's life.

The Hidden Work

A seed pushes roots down before it ever shows life above the ground.

Likewise, some of God's secrets are hidden because they're growing us first. God needs to teach us patience, trust, and humility. When the time is right, what He has hidden in the dark can then burst into the light.

Learning to Discern Seasons

Ecclesiastes reminds us there is a time for every purpose. Some answers come quickly. Some answers grow slowly. Some secrets may not be revealed until eternity.

Maturity trusts God with the *when*, not just the *what*. We place our prayers, needs, and desires into the hands of God, and then we turn them completely over to Him, both the answer and when we will receive it.

Your Due Season

Galatians 6:9 encourages:

Let us not grow weary in doing good, for at the proper time we will reap a harvest if we do not give up.

Our harvest comes at the proper time. The "when" is not up to us. God doesn't send the answer at "our" time, whether my time or your time, but at the perfect time.

Practical Ways to Trust God's Timing

Name the Wait

Write down what you're waiting for and give it back to God daily.

Water the Seed

While you wait, stay faithful. Keep praying. Keep loving. Keep obeying.

Watch for the Shoots

Be alert. When breakthrough comes, it often looks small at first.

Chapter 6

Revelation in Seasons

Reflection Questions

What secret thing are you waiting on God to reveal?

How is the waiting shaping you?

What does it mean to believe this phrase:

"Though it linger, wait for it"?

A Closing Prayer

Lord, teach me to trust Your seasons.

When waiting feels like silence, remind me You are working.

Help me see delay not as denial but as preparation.

Strengthen my faith to trust that in Your perfect time, every secret thing will bloom. Amen.

Challenge Yourself

Each morning, pray:

"Lord, I trust Your timing."

Write down one thing each day that you are waiting on from God.

At the end of each week, review your list for those needs that remain unanswered.

Choose to place them in God's hands and declare:

"In due season, God, You will provide everything that I need from You."

— 7 —

Living with Mystery

The Gift of Unknowing

Now faith is confidence in what we hope for and assurance about what we do not see.

— Hebrews 11:1 —

Living with Mystery

The Gift of Uncertainty

IF WE'RE HONEST, we'd rather have certainty than faith. We'd rather have clear answers than mystery.

But mystery isn't God's punishment. It's His gift.

It keeps our hearts soft. It keeps us humble.

And it keeps us longing for the day we see Him face to face.

A Clouded Mirror

Paul said:

For now we see only a reflection as in a mirror; then we shall see face to face.

— I Corinthians 13:12 —

In ancient times, mirrors were made of polished metal, meaning that they didn't show a perfect image.

They reflected shadows, hints, or outlines.

Life is like that. We see glimpses of what God is doing. We piece together meaning through His Word, His Spirit, and His promises.

The full picture is still coming, and it will be beautiful.

The Comfort of the Curtain

C.S. Lewis wrote that this world is only the shadowlands, that what we currently see is a mere outline of what's real and eternal.

Here's what Lewis meant by that:

God's secrets are like a curtain. Sometimes, He parts it just enough to let a small portion of His glory peek through. But much of who and what God is remains hidden.

His purpose is not to frustrate us but to keep us reaching. He desires us to see in Him the answer to our deepest needs and to search for His divine revelation in all things.

A Story: The Unfinished Chapter

Years ago, I spoke at a funeral for a young father. His wife asked me:

"Why did God let this happen?"

I told her the only thing I knew to say:

"I don't know why. But I know this isn't the last chapter."

Mystery reminds us that there is more to life than the physical things around us. This world is not the end.

The secret things whisper:

"You're not home yet."

Living with the Tension

To follow Jesus is to live with tension:

- Faith and Doubt

- Clarity and Confusion

- Hope and Unanswered Questions.

One day, the tension will break. We'll see the whole story. But for now, we trust in God and His divine plan for us.

When we place our trust in Him, our trust becomes a form of worship unto Him.

We are expressing our faith in His ability to care for us in the way that only He can.

Wonder Over Worry

Mystery can do two things:

- Feed worry.

- Fuel wonder.

Worry demands answers:

- Why?

- When?

- How?

Wonder says:

- Wow!

- Even here, God is good!

Children don't need to know everything about the universe to feel safe in their father's arms. The same is true for us. When we give our worry over to God, He gives us peace in exchange, and we rest in the safety of His care.

How to Live with Holy Mystery

Hold Questions Loosely

Some answers come in pieces, some in eternity. Keep asking - but don't let unanswered questions steal your peace.

Stay Anchored in What's Sure

When you can't see the full picture, stand on what you do know: He loves you. He's faithful. He's coming again.

Let Wonder Be Worship

When you bump into mystery, turn it into praise: "Lord, You are bigger than my mind can hold."

Chapter 7

Living with Mystery

Reflection Questions

What mystery have you struggled to surrender to God?

How could wonder replace your worry?

What truth about God helps you live with what you don't yet understand?

A Closing Prayer

Father, thank You for the mysteries I don't have to solve.

Thank You for what You've revealed and for what You've chosen to hold until the right time.

Keep my heart soft with wonder. Keep my faith strong in the gaps.

And remind me always that one day, I'll see You face to face. Amen.

Challenge Yourself

Sit with one big question you can't answer.

Pray:

"Lord, thank You for the secret things."

Search the Scriptures. Write down the references that best apply to your situation and keep them in your Bible.

Let God's unrevealed mystery draw you closer to His divine being instead of pushing you away.

A Final Word

You can find Tim on the South Texas District website at www.stxag.org, on Facebook, or at his Houston office when he's not traveling his home state ministering in the churches across the South Texas District.

He'd be thrilled to connect with you and share stories of God's faithfulness.

Additional Books by
Tim R. Barker

If you liked this book, you may be interested in additional books Tim has written. Turn the page for a short description of each book. All are available on Amazon.

My *Jesus* Journey

This soul-building, introspective 4-book series reveals Tim's innermost heart on subjects that affect all of us, from Cooperation to Loyalty to The Truth of Salvation and more.

The books in this series include:

My Jesus Journey
My Jesus Journey: Crescendo
My Jesus Journey: Glissando
My Jesus Journey: Rhapsody

At *Your* Feet

In this book, you will read of God's favor and His redemption, for you are chosen and forgiven. In Jesus, you can find the rest you desire, for at His feet, His joy becomes whole.

Come to Jesus today. He holds His hand out to you.

from the Book of Hebrews
The Lord with Us

Do you have a relationship with Jesus? The rewards are great, but if we fail to heed the warnings in the Word, the consequences are also great.

Even if we call ourselves Christian, we must live according to God's will. The Lord is with us when we walk with Him. This is the message from the book of Hebrews.

Philippians is our blueprint from the Father, our plan for joy. It was written by the hand of Paul during his time in a Roman prison, but the voice is the Father's, entreating us to lift our hands in praise to Him, and to find joy even in the difficult parts of our lives.

NAMES OF GOD

Our name tells people who we are.

What about the name Christian? That's what the followers of Jesus call themselves. What information can people glean about us when we put a fish symbol on the bumper of our car, or we wear a cross around our neck? And, importantly, do our actions live up to their expectations?

This book is an in-depth teaching about the ten names of God.

THE VISION OF
NEHEMIAH
GOD'S PLAN FOR RIGHTEOUS LIVING

The Book of Nehemiah reveals a vital truth that our instant society often overlooks. Determination can take us only so far in achieving the goals God has for today's Church.

Winning the lost for Christ takes preparation in both our time and our finances. We become the "right stuff" for achieving God's plan when we are willing to risk everything for Him.

GOD'S REVELATION AND YOUR FUTURE

The book of Revelation is first and foremost a revelation about Jesus, not just the future.

John reveals Christ as the King of Glory, the conqueror, the one in charge of history, the one who alone controls the future, controls the nations, controls all the universe! This is the Jesus who is coming!

The book of Revelation shows us the glorified Christ and the certainty of His ruling over all things. We are not stumbling toward an uncertain future, but we must be in fellowship with the King!

Truth, Love & Redemption

The Holy Spirit For Today

There is no greater empowerment for the Christian of today than to seek out the Holy Spirit. It was considered vital in the early days of Christendom. Now, many times it is pushed aside as "for then" and not "for now."

We are in greater need of the truth, love, and redemption that flows from an encounter with the Holy Spirit than ever before. The Scriptures tell us that our realization of our need for Christ flows from the Spirit. Even before we accept Christ, the Holy Spirit draws us to Him.

The *Call* of *Ephesians*

Building the Church of Today

Paul understood that legalism can become a hindrance to our Christian walk and that we must focus on Christ and Christ alone. When our faith hits the road, God is there with us. He challenges us to trust Him to walk at our side through every challenge we might face.

When we do, we become mighty warriors in God's army.

That's Paul's message in a nutshell, and it's vital we take it to heart.

The Twelve

Taking up the Mantle of Christ

Twelve men were chosen to fulfill Christ's legacy on the earth.

Eleven looked to Jesus for the answers to life's questions. One chose the world and the world failed him.

These men were as varied as the members of our modern church, at times at odds with one another, but forged by Jesus into a single unit that overcame everything the devil could throw at them. What lesson can we learn from them?

Our only option is to choose Christ.

END TIMES

Scripture provides us a timeline of events that signal that the end is coming soon.

1. The Church Age
2. The Rapture of the Church
3. The Tribulation
4. The Second Coming of Jesus Christ
5. The Millennium
6. The Great White Throne Judgment
7. New Heavens and New Earth

Follow along through each of these Biblical timeline events.

Anticipating the Return of Christ

Are we waiting or are we watching for His appearance in the skies? The difference is in being ready for His return and risking missing Him altogether.

This book covers six areas of preparation for the Return of Christ.

1. Waiting
2. Mindful
3. Joyful
4. Praying
5. Thanking
6. Faithful.

Are you anticipating Christ's return? I am.

I*Your*nvitation to*Christ*

Your Invitation to Christ guarantees six things. Once you accept Christ's invitation you can:

1. Rest. It's yours in the midst of whatever comes your way.
2. See. Your eyes are opened to the supernatural.
3. Follow. Christ is your only true leader.
4. Drink. The ambrosia of Jesus becomes yours.
5. Dine. You will find renewal in your fellowship with your Lord.
6. Inherit. The Kingdom will one day be yours. It's called Heaven.

Salvation comes through Christ. God desires our presence, and we draw closer to Him through our Lord and Savior, Jesus.

The Authentic Christian

Revealing Christ through the Fruit of the Spirit

How do we prove who we say we are?

What's the secret to how it's done?

Is it in appearance? Actions that portray honesty?

How do we live out our Christian example, prove that we are who we say we are? What's our authentication, our password, our photo ID?

That's what this book is about, how we can live a real and honest Christian life that reflects the truth of Jesus living through us.

When you finish this book, you will understand what it means to be an authentic Christian.

UNIFIED CHURCH

The world cries out for your leadership as a Christ-driven example of how to find security and safety in Him.

We must band together arm-in-arm, hand-in-hand, our thoughts, compassion, and commitment to each other linked for a common goal we all share: spreading the message of salvation to a world that desperately needs to see the example of Jesus lived out through committed believers.

This book will become a useful tool to focus your witness to those around you and strengthen your relationship to your family, your involvement in your local body of believers and your commitment to Christ.

Mighty Men of Courage

From the Bible

Joseph who was sold into slavery. Daniel faced the lion's den. Abraham saw few of the promises of God during his lifetime. Moses lived for four decades in disgrace, an apparent failure.

Elijah hid in the desert with the ravens for three years, and Paul was arrested for his faith and thrown in prison. Repeatedly.

Yet today we recognize these men as courageous examples of faith in God. The difference is that they took a stand for God, looked beyond their personal circumstances and in faith allowed the hand of God to lead them.

Christ is calling. I want to answer.

Join me today, won't you?

Open Doors

Inside or outside. That's what a door conveys.

We can choose to stand on one side or the other. We can keep things inside or outside, open the door or close it. Some doors are found in opportunities, worship, or faithfulness. Then there are emotional doors. We can be locked in or out. The doors become prison bars, trapping us in painful situations.

Death is the final door in this life. Do you dread it or look forward to what's on the other side?

This book is your opportunity to discover how the doors in your life align with the Word of God. The choice is yours: inside or outside?

Decide for Jesus today. He is the only choice worth making. Christ is calling.

I want to answer. Join me today, won't you?

Reflecting Christ

—— through the ——

Fruit
of the
Spirit

The reflection we cast. Does it reveal us or Christ?

There is a distinction between outward appearances and true substance, and it's clear in how we live out our lives as followers of Jesus.

Why would the world accept a Christian who doesn't live like Christ? That's where the Fruit of the Spirit comes into play in our lives.

How do we know the Fruit is active in our lives? We see it in the love we show to those in need.

Decide for Jesus today. He is the only choice worth making.

CALLED CAMP
—————2025—

Moses ... freeing the Egyptian slaves and parting the Red Sea!

David ... the King and the Psalmist!

Then there's Gideon, Jonah and Jeremiah!

Each of these men had to start somewhere small: Moses ran away to live in the desert. David tended sheep. Gideon, Jonah and Jeremiah just hoped to be left alone!

What has God called you to do for the kingdom? Are you willing to say yes?

Decide for Jesus today. He is the only choice worth making.

It's Not All About Sitting at the Head Table

Here's what the example of Jesus teaches us: branding isn't enough. Wearing the Christian name-tag is worthless if we don't hold up in the wash.

Do we feed the hungry? Do we clothe the naked? Are we a friend to the friendless and a comfort to the brokenhearted?

Jesus washed His disciples' feet. The Master stooped to the level of a servant, and in doing so, became a greater example of service than any soloist or evangelist ever dreamed.

The cost of leadership is heavy. The price for being "on show" rests hard on our shoulders.

Here's the lesson from our Lord:

To truly stand out in the Kingdom of God, we must first spend time on our knees.